Who ᴗares that
YOU CARE

Encouragement, Hope and Self-Care Tips

for Loving Yourself as You Care for

Someone with Dementia

Linda Michelle Trainer

Blessings
love + joy
Linda Michelle
Pro 3:-5-8
Feb 2020

Table of Contents

DEDICATIONS

"I have told you these things so that My joy

and delight may be in you and that your joy

may be made full and complete and overflowing." John 15:11 AMP

"Do not be anxious or worried about anything, but in everything (every circumstance
and situation) by prayer and petition with
thanksgiving, continue to make your (specific) requests known to God. And the peace
of God (that peace which reassures the heart,
that peace) which transcends all understanding, (that peace which) stands guard over
your hearts and your minds in

Christ Jesus (is yours)."

Philippians 4:6-8 Amplified Bible (AMP)

This book is dedicated to my precious sisters and brothers; Lisa Gail, Michael Matthew, Laurie Denise and Jeffrey Grand Alpasico. Thank you for your tangible, sacrificial expressions of love and care you continually show to our precious mama. Thank you for your willingness to plan together, to pray together and to prepare together as a family on her behalf. Houston Alpasico would be very proud.

Thanksgiving 2017

Thanksgiving 2019

To my precious nephew Tommie Preston, your dedication to your grandma during this season of her life is priceless. To share space and time, to help protect her and keep her comfortable and happy even through the backlash and "dementia drama", is a gift our family values far more than you will ever know. Your bond with your grandma is unbreakable, even though some of her memories are faded. She was in the delivery room when you were born. You are forever in her heart. You are forever in our heart, with overflowing gratitude and thanksgiving.

To "Ally" (Alexandria), the best caregiver this side of heaven. Thank you for stepping in and helping to care for our mama as if she were a part of your own family from the very beginning. We all pray God's continued blessings of abundance, peace and joy in your life.

To Madeleine Carol's grandchildren, great grands, nieces, nephews, sisters, brothers and cousins, in-laws and friends, she has photo picture proof of her love for you, which can never be erased from her heart.

To my uncle Bob Evans, thank you for being the voice of wisdom and encouragement, offering your prayers and counsel to stand strong in doing what we knew was best for Mama, even in her resisting. Thank you for your strong arms of comfort, for drying my tears and praying with me through my fears. I praise God for the gift of you to our family.

To my husband, thank you, from the depths of my heart, for allowing me space to care for Mama; to be away and process when I need and welcoming me back with unconditional love. Thank you for being my soft place to rest. J t'aime.

"It is one of the most beautiful compensations of life, that no man can sincerely try to help another without helping himself."
 ~ Ralph Waldo Emerson

We do not come to this earth with an owner's

 Manuel, however if we did it would be

"Who Cares that You Care". Linda Michelle

Trainer is a gifted writer who has created a

masterful guide to self-care for caregivers of

loved ones challenged with Alzheimer's Dis-

ease or Dementia! A first of its kind, must

read!

Alise Jones-Bailey M.D.

It's crazy how much I miss the old you, grandma. I look back and cherish times I had with you. I know you're not the same and you may not remember who I am but I love you so much and you will always be my loving, picture taking, poem writing, beautiful grandma.~McCaylah

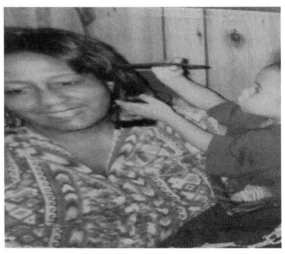

Precious memory of McCaylah combing her grandma's hair

FOREWORD

Linda Michelle, one of my spiritual daughters, and one whom I have had both the honor
and privilege of mentoring and sharing with
for more than 20 years, as well as being her
friend, has written a phenomenal work sharing her vast experience of learning to care for
herself appropriately while serving as caregiver to others. I love her transparency and
honesty of the journey she has been traveling
with her mother who has transitioned from a
diagnosis of Dementia into now what appears
to be full-blown Alzheimer's.

As I have followed this journey with Linda, I
remember a few years back when she first began to share with me what was happening
with her mother, neither of us knew at the

time the extent of it, nor the length of the journey. This book Linda has written is probably one of the most important books I will read for this year, 2019, primarily because I've seen some of the same cognitive decline symptoms exhibited in my husband of almost 38 years and it helps me to understand so much of what I have not known before now. As the data illustrates, millions upon millions of people are diagnosed with and even die from this heinous disease, but most of us do not think a lot about our loved ones or even ourselves being stricken with it. We often make jokes about having "senior moments" or "brain fog/freeze," but if we only knew the debilitating effects that comes with Dementia or Alzheimer's we would not joke so easily about our brain.

Before reading Linda's manuscript, I had already delved into my own research and discovered both Dementia and Alzheimer's disease is preventable as well as reversible; most people are not aware of this fact. Some of you may have read my book The Whole Soul concerning care of our mind, thoughts, and the brain, and if so, you will understand why this is such a passionate concern of mine. I feel very strongly that until we learn how to read and understand the messages of our own bodies, we cannot be the effective caregivers we need to be. I hear so many stories of the anger, abuse and "mean-spiritedness" people exhibit when caring for their loved ones, whether it is a parent, child, sibling, spouse, or even close friend or relative. Much of this is a direct result, one of our own selfishness, and two, because we simply are tired, afraid, and have not learned to care for our own emotional, physical, and even spiritual needs.

Who Cares That You Care is not about the disease itself, although Linda provides her reading audience with great background data and statistics; but it is written primarily to the caregiver—the persons like you and me who have not given much thought to how we are to care for ourselves during crisis, such as providing care for the person stricken with some type of illness or disease. It is imperative to follow the Biblical mandate from Jesus for advancing the Kingdom. He tells the disciples in the 16th chapter of Mark, verse 15b "…Go everywhere and announce the message of God's good news to one and all!" In order for us to adhere to this very significant mandate we must be certain to care for our own needs, otherwise the good news, being representative not just of salvation, but peace, wholeness, and soundness of mind, will somehow get lost in the going. To properly care for and extend genuine love to someone who has become incapacitated, requires our properly taking care of ourselves. It is very difficult to have soundness of mind when one is stressed, anxious, worried, scared, or even angry about caring for a loved one.

Bravo to you Linda. In writing this very insightful, profound, yet easily comprehensible manual, Who Cares That You Care, you have provided us with the tools--through implementing very easy steps, necessary to make sure caregivers are of soundness of mind, not anxious or worried, and definitely not angry. I wholeheartedly believe this book will be an eye opener for many who have not yet learned to love ourselves, despite our thinking we already know how to "care for our-selves." We often exercise, eat properly, and even get enough sleep. However, when we are called upon to do many of those things for someone other than ourselves that might not be such an easy undertaking. Many of us have raised children, cared for them when they were ill, and yet, caring for a person who has lost the ability to care for themselves is an al-together different scenario.

As Kingdom citizens we must learn the art of loving ourselves; that comes with under-standing the depth of God's love for His sons and daughters. As we understand this whole concept of love, we realize yes it is our re-sponsibility to love others, but at the same time we must learn to care enough about our-selves that when we are called upon to genu-inely and unconditionally love others, there is enough love within us to spill over onto others. As Linda so eloquently refers to it in her book, "allow our saucers to overflow..."

My prayer is that this book becomes one of the most important books on your library shelf. Though its specific topic is Dementia, speaking volumes to us about caring for others, but also remembering not to relinquish our responsibility to care for ourselves – in other words, put the oxygen mask over our face first—then and only then can we faithfully, lovingly, and effortlessly care for someone else.

Gayle Rogers, Ph.D., Author, Motivational Speaker, Coach Mental Health Practitioner, Founder & CEO, Forever Free, Inc. &

Coaching for Empowerment

INTRODUCTION

It has been said that one of the most difficult tasks women have is learning how to practice self-love. When you're also a survivor of a past trauma such as incest or sexual abuse, domestic violence, poverty or addiction, learning to love yourself can be challenging yet it is also key to your healing journey.

Throw your mother's diagnosis of Dementia into the mix on top of your own healing journey from past trauma and BAM! It can feel like you have been side-swiped by a 787 jet liner while sitting at a traffic stop.

Yet, even inside of the seemingly impossible situations, life is still happening. The blood is still running warm in your veins; your mind - although in a tailspin – is still processing thoughts; your heart is still beating with vibrant life. And your love for your loved one with dementia is demanding more from you than you believe you can handle.

What do you do? Where do you begin? How do you help someone you love while you are trying to make sure that all of the pieces to your mental ability are still in tack? For those who have experienced past trauma or not, the answer remains the same:

You begin by loving you.

Whether you have experienced a past trauma, have come through a divorce or death of a close relative or friend, a loved one with dementia needs your help. They deserve the best of you that you have to give. You deserve to give yourself the best of you to yourself first, and then to your loved one.

This book offers you tips and strategies that will benefit you where you are, here and now; it will help to guide you through the maze into the place you desire to be – a "Shero" to your loved one with dementia.

Give yourself permission to take time to investigate what it is I am sharing in this book. If the information fits, apply it to your life; implement the strategies and tips suggested; receive the hope and encouragement. Reach out to me to dive deeper into tools and resources that will further help you to help yourself, as you help your loved one with dementia.

If this does not apply to you, I hope you are at least inspired with ideas that were sparked by something you read. If not for you, please pass this book along or share the link. In my research it appears there is a correlation between past trauma, especially of childhood sexual abuse and caregiver of loved ones with dementia. The Alzheimer's Association has found there were an estimated 46.8 million people world-wide living with Dementia in 2015. According to the Center for Disease Control (CDC) more than 1 in 3 women experience sexual violence involving physical contact during her lifetime. Nearly 1 in 4 men experienced sexual violence involving physical contact during his lifetime. Someone inside your circle of influence will be able to relate and apply this information and they will be eternally grateful to you for sharing.

But most importantly, you would have taken some time out to show yourself a form of self-love, in the simplest way.

CHAPTER 1 PRAISE/PRAY: TAP INTO YOUR SPIRITUAL GPS FOR PERSONAL GUIDANCE

"The thing that is really hard and really amazing, is giving up on being perfect, and beginning the work of becoming yourself."
Anna Quindlen

"Self-care is never a selfish act – it is simply good stewardship of the only gift I have, the gift I was put on earth to offer to others." ~
Parker Palmer

This book is written for you.

I CARE ABOUT YOU as you go about caring for your loved one or friend with dementia.

I CARE ABOUT YOU as you care for a loved one who has had a stroke, heart attack, who has ALS/Lou Gehrig's disease, S/Muscular Dystrophy/Autism.

I CARE ABOUT YOU as you care for those in your life and sphere of influence who need your wisdom, your strength, your efforts and your prayers.

I CARE ABOUT YOU because I am familiar with your journey. I have walked a similar path.

Just as no two finger-prints are exactly alike, no two care giving situations are inch for inch alike. However, just as our fingers are the common denominator when talking about our finger-prints, the foundational emotional, physical and mental toll that it takes to care for another human being who is limited in the care they can give to themselves, is identical.

I have experienced caring for my great aunt after she had a stroke; I have assisted with the care of my grandmother after she had a mastectomy and then a few short months later developed Alzheimer's; I was blessed to help care for my precious mother-in-law and I am currently assisting in the care of my precious mama, whose diagnosis of dementia was just recently updated to a diagnosis of Alzheimer's.

I have gained unwanted, yet necessary wisdom inside of situations that I wish were not mine to experience. I have learned how to navigate through hot tears of disbelief and crazy confusion; choking frustration and bone aching weariness; fuming anger and then to a retreating surrender and reluctant acceptance. Acceptance that this "dementia drama" too shall pass, yet right here right now I have an opportunity to make a difference, sow seeds of love and encouragement and allow God to use me to bring even the smallest amount of joy and comfort to those I love and adore, before they themselves pass.

This book is about caring for and loving yourself as you care for a loved one with Dementia. For some it will be a reminder. For others it is an introductory guide back to themselves. For all it will be a strategic plan or a "map" to begin an overlooked process in your life.

The self-care strategies, encouragement, hope and self-care tips I have included within this short, easy to read and implement resource, can be applied to any general caregiving situation on the planet. I have chosen to focus on self-care inside the arena of caring for a loved one with Dementia to impart help to one of the most overlooked populations currently.

According to the Family Caregiver Alliance, approximately 43.5 million caregivers have provided unpaid care to an adult or child in the last 12 months. The National Alliance for Caregiving and AARP have reported that about 34.2 million Americans have provided unpaid care to an adult age 50 or older in the last 12 months.

So that we have a clear understanding, allow me to share what I mean by Dementia.

The Center for Disease Control (CDC) states that "Dementia is not a specific disease but is rather a general term of impaired ability to remember, think, or make decisions that interfere with doing everyday activities.

Alzheimer's disease is the most common type of dementia. Though dementia mostly affects older adults, it is not part of normal ageing."

The World Health Organization adds "Dementia is a syndrome, usually of a chronic or progressive nature –in which there is deterioration in cognitive function (i.e. the ability to process thought) beyond what might be expected from normal ageing. It affects memory, thinking, orientation, comprehension, calculation, learning capacity, language, and judgement. Consciousness is not affected. The impairment in cognitive function is commonly accompanied, and occasionally preceded, by deterioration in emotional control, social behavior, or motivation.

Dementia results from a variety of diseases and injuries that primarily or secondarily affect the brain, such as Alzheimer's disease or stroke."

Some Key Facts are:

• Dementia is a syndrome in which there is deterioration in memory, thinking, behavior and the ability to perform everyday activities.

• Although dementia mainly affects older people, it is not a normal part of ageing.

• Worldwide, around 50 million people have dementia, and there are nearly 10 million new cases every year.

• Alzheimer disease is the most common form of dementia and may contribute to 60-70% of cases.

• Dementia is one of the major causes of disability and dependency among older people worldwide.

• Dementia has a physical, psychological, social, and economic impact, not only on people with dementia, but also on their carers (caregivers), families and society at large. (WHO.INT)

The World Health Organization explains the risk factor and prevention strategies this way:

"Although age is the strongest known risk factor for dementia, it is not an inevitable consequence of ageing. Further, dementia does not exclusively affect older people – young onset dementia (defined as the onset of symptoms before the age of 65) accounts for up to 9% of cases. Studies show that people can reduce their risk of dementia by getting regular exercise, not smoking, avoiding harmful use of alcohol, controlling their weight, eating a healthy diet, and maintaining healthy blood pressure, cholesterol and blood sugar levels. Additional risk factors include

depression, low educational attainment, social isolation and cognitive inactivity."
(emphasis are mine)

"…Dementia can be overwhelming for families of affected people and for their carers (caregivers).

Physical, emotional, and financial pressures can cause great stress to families and carers (caregivers), and support is required from health, social, financial and legal systems."
(who.int)

The "struggle" is real. The heartaches, disbelief, and the anger at the disease is real. The living grief is real. Having my mother deny she is actually my mother, and hearing her argue that her son is not her son, but she is convinced he is her brother, brings sadness to my heart. The weariness of hearing my mother ask the same question at least "10 times in 30 seconds", and me having to answer in love, each and every time as if it were the very first, is real.

Having my precious mama, who used to have on her lipstick and her "hair" even before she got out of bed in the mornings since my child-hood days, now refuse to take a bath or shower – angrily arguing that she just did, the day before, when it has actually been weeks – is real! What is even more real is the life and death reality that you must care for your-self first and fully, so that you can lovingly, patiently and effectively care for that person you love.

It is absolutely vital that you fill your cup so that you will be able to meet the needs of your loved one, at the same time as sustaining your energy and focus to take care of yourself and your needs that you have aside from your loved one. Times of celebration, praise and thanksgiving can help to reduce your stress level and re-adjust and renew your mind set.

What is Self-Care? According to PsychCentral, "Self-Care is an activity that we do deliberately in order to take care of our mental, emotional and physical health. Good self-care is key to improved mood, and reduced anxiety. It's also key to good relationship with oneself and others."

Self-care is also defined as maintaining your health through health-promoting practice. According to the Royal Australasian College of Physicians, it involves "looking after your needs, on a daily basis and times of crisis in order to maintain a positive emotional, psychological and physiological resilience and well-being."

According to the American Psychological Association, adults living in the United States reported a higher level of stress in 2015 compared to 2007. A significant number of individuals also stated that the stress had impacted them physically and mentally, and had developed headaches, felt anxious or depressed. As a result, some of their behavior changes included yelling at loved one, cancelling social plans and ignoring responsibilities."

Self-care is a personal matter, and it is vitally imperative that every person care for themselves.

I know firsthand how challenging this is to do on a regular basis. We could spend a full day or more comparing details on just the time it takes to accomplish even the basic things it takes to just get through one portion of the day with our loved ones we care for. With that in mind, it is absolutely essential that you are fully equipped to handle all that is involved in caring for your loved one.

In addition to eating healthy, exercising, having regular medical and dental check-ups and making time for fun and joy in your life, a simple, first things first step to making time for self-care is to tap into what I call your Spiritual GPS: God's Power System for personal guidance.

Regardless of your religious background, spirituality is about relationship rather than customs and habits. Similar to the GPS - Global Positioning Satellite systems installed in our cell phones, cars and watches, that helps us to know where we are going and how to get there, your Spiritual GPS: God's Power System is more than capable of directing and protecting your journey. It is activated by faith and implementation of God's Word. It begins with acknowledgement of His Presence and acceptance of His gifts of supply in every form needed.

In the beginning was God. And we are now here on this journey of caring for our loved one with Dementia, and God is still here. It is not by accident or coincidence. Nor is it by Divine Design that sickness and disease invade our minds and bodies or the bodies of our loved one, without His Comforting Presence and Love with us.

There are human factors that have interfered with the ultimate Divine Design of Almighty God, which is for health, wholeness and peace of mind (see John 10:10, Roman 15:13 & John 8:12). Yet, He is with us. Access to the help, wisdom and power that will successfully take us through the caring process of our loved one is readily available for the asking and receiving.

I have found myself on many occasions crying out to God for what to do when my mother switches from speaking in loving tones to me and suddenly goes into a rampage, insisting that I tell her who my "real mother" is. I can almost see her blood pressure rise as she boils with anger at me for "lying to her" as I calmly repeat to her that I am indeed her daughter and that she is my mother.

I have resulted to pointing to the family pictures we have displayed around her apartment. That may or may not settle it for her. What I am often left with is another example of how my precious mother, who was once my greatest cheerleader and encourager; my mama that has told me since I was riding a bicycle with training wheels, that I was "made in love"; this same lady has now completely forgotten that I am her own flesh and blood. Forgotten for at least that moment in time.

Maybe tomorrow will be different. Maybe the "clouds" of confusion will part and maybe the "sun" will come out tomorrow and she will remember that I am her "other favorite" child that she gave birth to. Only the supernatural love of God can heal a heart from such desperate disappointment and pain. I have cried out many times in prayer for God's help. He has never failed to answer me.

I recently came across a powerful scripture that seals my love and trust in God and reveals His steadfast, passionate love for me:

"So the Lord answers, "Can a woman forget her own baby and not love the child she bore?

Even if a mother should forget her child, I will never forget you Jerusalem (Linda Michelle,) I can never forget you! I have written your name on the palm of My Hands."
Isaiah 49:15 (GNT version)

There is no magic formula required. A simple "Jesus, please help me. Come into my heart and mind and activate Your Wisdom in and through me" is an example of how simple it is to tap into your Spiritual GPS: God's Power System for personal guidance.

On the matter of prayer, it has been said that "…Prayer is not a method we use to convince God about a matter. Neither do we pray hoping that if we pray long enough we can manipulate God to give us what we want. Neither does prayer mean begging God and hoping that He will finally have mercy on us and hear our prayer.

No, Prayer means that we position ourselves in a way that allows God to fulfill His plans. We thus enable God to fulfill His plans, the things that Jesus paid the price for 2,000 years ago. We become part of His Salvation plan by aligning our lives in prayer with the principles of God."

(From Redeeming Your Bloodline: Foundations for Breaking Generational Curses from the Courts of Heaven by Hrvoje Sirovina and Robert Henderson)

The question has been asked by Mark Batterson, author of Draw the Circle: The 40 Day Prayer Challenge, "can our prayers change our circumstances? Absolutely! But when our circumstances don't change, it's often an indication that God is trying to change us. The primary purpose of prayer is not to change circumstances: the primary purpose of prayer is to change us! But either way, the chief objective remains the same: to glorify God in any and every situation. Sometimes God delivers us from our problems; sometimes God delivers us through our problems."

The scripture which inspired the words I wrote in my inspirational CD "Be IN Courage" is something I also pray often. I invite you to pray with me here and now, if you would like, applying this to your life, as I declare the scripture, "Let the morning bring me Word of Your unfailing Love, for I have put my trust in You. Show me the way I should go, for to You I lift up my soul." (Psalm 143:8, NIV)

My hope and my prayer is that the encouragement, inspiration of hope, tips, and information provided in this book will help you to find effective ways to, "… seize and hold fast and retain without wavering the hope we cherish and confess..." (Hebrews 10:23) helping and equipping YOU to care for YOU better, so that you can provide the best possible care for the one you love and serve.

I am united with you in purpose, on purpose, for God's purpose, with love.

CHAPTER 2 PAMPER: OVERFLOW YOUR CUP AND SERVE FROM YOUR SAUCER

"Taking care of yourself doesn't mean me first, it means me too." ~ L.R. Krost

You would not be able to read this book electronically if your device had no charge. In a similar manner, you will not be able to "read" or care for your loved one without having replenished your energy and strength. You will not be fully in tune to their needs, which they themselves don't realize they have.

Several years ago I found myself out of tune with my own needs on a major scale. I had an experience that proved to be "the worse, best thing" that could have ever happened to give me a clear understanding of the importance of rest and taking care of yourself.

In March of 2007 I spent thirteen days in a mental health facility after being misdiagnosed as being bi-polar. What I actually had was adrenal fatigue, also known as adrenal exhaustion. The adrenals are two small glands that sit on top of your kidneys. Their job is to regulate your stress hormones, primarily adrenaline and cortisol. The adrenal glands give you increased focus and stamina to deal with sudden situations that require your full attention and effort.

To cope with the stressors and strains on the body, your adrenal glands faithfully pump out extra energy to you. Adrenal fatigue occurs when the adrenals reach the point where they are barely functioning. Some of the symptoms appear as extreme fatigue, depression, frequent illnesses, hormone imbalance and the inability to cope with stressful situations when they arise.

To help me understand what was happening, my doctor (the very wise and competent Dr. Alise Jones-Bailey) used the analogy of my body being like a car that was empty of gasoline. She said that I was forcing it to move, pressing relentlessly on the accelerator and paying no attention to its needs.

During that time in my life, I was going full force, trying to tend to all the pressing needs around me. There was the increased stress in my job and commute as a flight attendant, as well as a growing demand for services and training in my non-profit organization. My husband was going through a major change in his career and my father was diagnosed with terminal cancer, and I was summoned and served a 3-month term of Grand Jury duty.

I was overwhelmed and stressed beyond the max! My body was depleted, and did not know how to slow down. I was beyond tired. I was completely drained and I didn't recognize it.

I also did not fully implement the clear instruction of my doctor, who had blood and saliva test evidence that I needed to take recommended supplements, from a compound pharmacy, continue eating a healthy diet (at the time I was following the South Beach Diet) and to continue with exercise at least 3 times per week (at time all I could fit into my schedule was the 8 minute Tae Bo exercises, but it was working.)

I had a clear, concise recommended strategy, with documented evidence to back it up, but I didn't follow suit. I let my "but" get in the way: "But I don't have time, But I don't have the energy, But I don't have the money…" Not implementing the wisdom of my doctor landed my "butt" in a place that I didn't want to be. I had been serving from my "cup", instead of from an overflow and my "cup" was bone dry.

The days in isolation in the hospital came as a blessing in disguise, and my life transitioned for the better. I experienced an awakening that could not have come to me in any other way. I ate three healthy meals each day. I spent at least thirty minutes outside in the sun daily and was in bed by nine o'clock every night. That alone was miraculous. I had not followed that kind of routine in years.

Eventually, my body and brain were able to rest, and my mind became sharper than ever. I gained valuable insight and understanding.

Before my time in the hospital, when first diagnosed with Adrenal fatigue and entering perimenopause, with blood tests to prove it, I was given a recommended diet to follow, a list of supplements to take (from a compound pharmacy), and strict instructions to reduce my stress levels and implement exercise and rest into my daily regime.

I didn't implement the instructions for what I thought were several "good reasons:" I had to work the hours to keep my job and earn the extra money to buy the recommended supplements that I needed; I also had to take time to visit my daddy (who lived in a different state from where I lived, which was a different state from where I worked and was based) to see how I could help him.

At the same time, I was being asked to share my experience, speaking and coaching services to help teen girls who had experienced incest and sexual abuse, at a weekend retreat and a major convention that was being planned in my home city.

These were all "good reasons" right? Yes, they were, however they were the "good" reasons at the "wrong" time for the condition of my body. I was putting my health on the back burner as I attempted to carry on business as usual.

Not heeding the advice of my highly skilled and well paid doctor – who gave me a copy of the blood test she made her recommendations from – led me straight to the emergency room, where a doctor, who did not have access to my blood test results, and refused to even hear me discuss my doctor who did, because she was an integrative GYN. He was only looking at the aftermath of burn-out, mixed with hormonal imbalance and overload, layered under a mountain of total exhaustion.

Instead of calling my GYN to even question if what I was explaining to him was valid, he told my husband that I was bi-polar and that I had been religiously brain-washed and should be treated at a mental facility for at least the recommended 72 hour hold. That 72 hours turned into 13 days of a time of clarity.

I discovered God was truly God all by Himself and He didn't need my help. I was not "Holy Ghost, Jr". It turned out to be a time of refreshing rest and a time of encouragement and validation that God does use me as His vessel, as some of the other patients came to me asking me to pray for them. Their request seemed to come out of the blue. God had restored what the enemy meant for evil and He worked it together for my good.

After I returned to work, several people, many with tears in their eyes, spoke of how they could personally relate to my story. It promoted several of them to visit their doctors to have their own testing done.

By the way, the threat the emergency room psychiatrist made to my husband that if I were to stop taking the Psychiatric drugs and anti-depression medication he had prescribed would cause another relapse which would be 10 times worse than the first proved to be untrue.

Not being able to function without feeling as if I was starring in a re-looping, slow motion scene in a Twilight Zone episode, 24 hours/7 days a week, I shared with my husband, my mother and my sister, who was a registered nurse, that I was going to wean myself off all of the medication.

Although my husband was boiling over with anger at the idea of me possibly having a relapse like the doctor had shared with him, my mother and sister both advised me to carefully monitor my condition, being careful to see the doctor if I needed, as well as urging me to continue to pray and hear God's direction, for Whom they trusted inside of me.

In just a few short weeks the medication was out of my system and from that day in 2007 till today, over twelve years later, I have never had any adverse reaction from the withdrawal, nor have I ever even come close to being or exhibiting signs of being bi-polar.

I share these personal details with you in the hope that you will use it as a checklist to evaluate your life and make the changes that are necessary for your optimal well-being.

DO CONSULT YOUR PHYSICIAN BEFORE DISCONTINUING ANY PRESCRIBED MEDICATION.

With awareness and understanding comes power. Power is the ability or capacity to act or perform effectively.

Self-care honors your mind and body as the gifts they are.

As a caregiver of someone with dementia, you have become their "instinct" of sorts. You are often able to sense what they need even before they realize they need it. In the state of Adrenal Fatigue that my body experienced in 2007, I could not have been an effective help to my daddy in my own weakened state.

We have to have a full cup from which we can draw from in order to help others. You are fearfully and wonderfully made – engineered for success, which requires replenishment on several different levels, physically, mentally and emotionally.

I have heard one of my coaches and sister in the journey, Lisa Nichols share the following in person and in recordings a few hundred times over, in one form or another: "You must serve from your saucer instead of from your cup." In a portion of one of her online recordings entitled "Loving Yourself" she shares her wisdom on the subject in this way:

"Someone's going to cross your path tomorrow, next week, next year and they need the love that you have, but in order for them to get it, you need to have filled your cup up and you need to be an overflow, because you can't love them from your cup, you got to always love them from your saucer.

Yes, because when you love them from your saucer you never, ever run out; you never love on an empty tank; love never hurts. A lot of time when love is hurting it's because you haven't given you everything you need yet. And you're trying to give other people what you still need. You're trying to give them your oxygen (mask) which is why you're sitting around (gasping for air) going "hurry up."

Recognize that when you love from your overflow that's the most responsible thing that you could do. And that the greatest love that you can ever give the world is the demonstration of what loving you looks like:

If she can give herself 1,000 second chances, then I can give myself one more. And if he can give himself another chance, if he can get up after that financial fall,

If he can get up after that divorce,

If she can get up after that break up,

If he can get back up after having to leave his children,

If she can get back up after having that child,

If she can define herself then what can I do?

So, your demonstration of how madly in love with you you are helps me to recognize how madly in love with me I get to be.

And then, when I love myself enough then all my extra just oozes over onto you.

And when you let your light shine like that, because you've fallen in love with you, all of a sudden you get in the corner and that light for a moment brightens up someone's momentary darkness and then you've been a blessing to someone else."

Bravo and a soul stirring thank you to you Lisa Nichols for sharing this wisdom of "Loving Yourself" in such a profound and relatable way.

Bravo and an equally soul stirring thank you to YOU for caring as much as you do for your loved one with dementia. Thank you for now reaffirming a commitment to yourself to love and care for yourself, even more so, that you will be around a whole lot longer to continue to care for your loved one; that the world will

be blessed with the gift of the presence of
your brilliance.

CHAPTER 3 PLAN: MAP OUR YOUR PROPOSED DESIRES WITH SPACE FOR DETOURS

"Self-care is taking all the pressures you are facing right now, and deciding to which you will respond, and how." Imani Shola

The care for my mother is a team effort. One of my precious sisters and I share Guardianship and Conservatorship. Since she lives in the same city as Mama (about 10 minutes away), she handles the medication and medical aspect for her, and I handle the financial end. Since most of the financial affairs can be conducted over the internet, I am not restricted by living out of state. I am blessed to be able to travel to be with my mom several times a month. Even if for 2 days I can replenish needed groceries, wash clothes, change bedding and spend time with Mama, relieving my sister and my nephew.

My nephew has unselfishly agreed to live with his grandma to help be the "eyes and ears" for our family, helping to keep her safe and comfortable. Even though he does work outside of the house, as well as being a technological entrepreneur, his presence in the apartment with our mama (with a separate bedroom and separate bathroom), allows us a sense of peace of mind that we would not have without him.

The help of my other siblings is invaluable. Our middle sister, who is also caring for one of our aunts, and one of our brothers travels the hour distance to spend time with mama; taking her out to dinner on occasion or just simply spending quality time with her. Our youngest brother has been a huge help in handling Mama's house and property, as well as traveling 3 hours from his home to also spend quality time with and cook for Mama.

We have telephone conference calls, as well as face to face meetings when the need arises to discuss as a family what next steps to take and deciding on how to contribute – financially or physically. Each of my siblings are married and my "other sisters and brothers" as I affectionately call my in-laws, contribute just as much, in the care of my mama, by allowing time and space, as well as financial resources to be allocated from their personal family time and budget to help.

Just as I am thankful for my husband for accepting this journey and contributing in the same manner as my in-laws, I am forever grateful. My mother's children could not do all that we do for her without the support and unconditional love of our spouses. (Thank you all!! God bless you 100-fold.)

Although your family structure may be different, Be IN courage by the example of how responsibilities and duties can be shared as you care for your loved ones. There is help available, either from inside your family circle or from an outside agency.

Know that you do not have to walk the path alone.

As part of my flight attendant training I am taught to be "situationally aware." Situational awareness is being aware of what is happening in the vicinity around you, in order to understand how "information, events and one's own actions will impact goals and objectives, both immediately and in the near future."

You can improve your situational awareness which can be adapted to your own care and the care of your loved one by implementing these tips:

• Learn to predict events:

Plan extra preparation time in your schedule before appointments or outings if your loved one requires additional time to dress, bathe or freshen up when getting ready. This simple act will save incredible loads of stress on you and your loved one.

Also be attentive to the mood of your loved one with dementia. If this is the third time in a row that she refuses to get out of the car after you return from an outing, perhaps she wants to spend more time with you and not let your time together end so quickly, even if it has been a full day.

- Identify elements around you

Dress both of you appropriately for the weather; pack and take additional set of clothes and Depends (adult briefs) with you for your loved one in case of an unexpected accident. Secure and stow sharp knives, weapons and objects that will harm your loved one or which could be used by your loved one to harm others; put away pictures that trigger negative feelings and behavior.

- Limit situational overload

Do not plan for more errands or activities than you can handle when traveling around town, or even out of town with your loved one. On a crowded flight from San Francisco back to Detroit a year ago, my mother sat at the window seat and refused to take her assigned middle or even my aisle seat. Thank God the flight was not oversold and the passenger assigned the window was gracious and understanding enough to take another open seat.

This incident happened shortly after me losing my mom at that same airport, just prior to boarding the same flight with the seat situation, when she didn't make it back from her solo trip to the restroom. We both were tired and ready to be back in Detroit.

Turn off the TV, stereo and/ or computer if your loved one is being agitated by the sound. Beware of the "clicking" sounds your key board makes when typing on your computer, as well as the "bing" sounds when you post or receive a post from social media.

The super-sensitivity of our loved ones with dementia is often disturbed by sounds and noises we often overlook or take for granted.

- Trust your Feelings

Postpone that walk around the block or apartment complex parking lot, even if it has been longer than usual at being inside. An unforeseen mishap could be avoided.

By the same token, when your loved one suddenly asks to go for a walk, confirm inner peace within yourself about it and do not hesitate.

Don't even take time to brush your teeth or comb your own hair or groom your loved one. The fleeting desire may pass just as suddenly as it arose. Swish some mouthwash in your mouth, grab the nearest hat or scarf and proceed to enjoy the well-deserved fresh air outside and watch the smiles light up on your loved one's face.

•   Avoid complacency:

Assuming everything is under control will affect your vigilance. You have to actively keep yourself in the right mindset. Your loved one with dementia will experience a rollercoaster of emotions throughout the day, even moment by moment, which can look different each day.

Ensuring their bedroom window is closed on cold nights, for the fourth time in one night is a real concern. Watching what your loved one picks up when out visiting or when there are things lying around that don't belong to them.

My mother has a tendency to hide things, in one of her many handbags; in between the pillows of the sofa or even in the back portion of the top drawer of her night stand. After searching for the TV remote for a couple of weeks and my sister putting it at the bottom of her long list of concerns, I just happened to find it in the back portion of a very deep drawer of her night stand, when looking for a hand mirror my mother requested while sitting on the sofa.

Just this Thanksgiving, she was showing me things from her handbag after we arrived at her apartment from dinner with our family, one of which was an electronic tablet. She was very upset when I quickly took it from her, yet I knew it was not hers. I had to take time allotted for rest to send a group text to ask the family who was missing their tablet.

The next morning when Mama was in the living room and her purse was still in the bedroom, I did a quick search and found a magnifying glass that belonged to my brother-in-law; the tablet belonged to my sister, who uses it every day!

Had I not noticed what my mama was showing me and tuning into what she was saying to me, even though I was weary and preparing for bed, we may have not discovered the missing tablet for weeks or months.

Making sure they are not applying Bengay cream to their body when they desire to put body lotion on themselves.

Minor things can quickly become major concerns. Even waking early so you can shower, brush your teeth and comb your hair before your loved one wakes will keep you prepared for the sudden desire to go for a walk, as mentioned above. The peace of mind of a fresh breath and combed hair are priceless little treasures that add up to help reduce your stress levels in tremendous ways.

- Be aware of time

Keep watch of the times your loved one eats and sleeps. This will not only help you to gauge a good time for you to sleep and rest, it will also help you to help your loved one monitor their food intake, as well as help you notice changes in their behavior, mood or health.

My nephew was having dinner with his grandma one evening when he noticed that the conversation became erratic and non-comprehensible. He called his mom who quickly came over to discover that something was "not right."

Precious time was taken trying to convince my mother to get into the car so she could be taken to the hospital or urgent care. Because mama refused the paramedics had to be called. She had to be strapped to a gurney in order to get her out of the apartment.

At the hospital Mama refused to allow the CT Scan procedure to be performed, which would have identified what had taken place in her body. Her strong will and tenacious stubbornness (intensified by the dementia) was surrendered to. The doctor explained they would not have been able to do anything except monitor her regardless of what the test may have revealed.

My sister, being led by wisdom from her experience as a trained emergency room nurse and confirmation from the doctor, and peace from Holy Spirit, all seasoned with love for her 79-year-old mother, put a cease to the fighting Mama was doing with the hospital staff, took her home and monitored her personally.

Thank God Mama has not had any other similar episodes. She has since been examined thoroughly by a geriatrician, an appointment moved several months forward from a 6 month waiting list, because of the urgency of the hospital visit- truly a blessing in disguise.

• Begin to evaluate and understand situations

Check in with yourself several times throughout the day to sense how you are doing. H.A.L.T., and ask yourself are you Hungry, Angry, Lonely or Tired. Take time to address your needs which surface. Monitor your loved one's tone of voice or body language when in the company of others, as well as others interactions with your loved one.

• Continually assess the situation

Stay vigilant, physically, emotionally and spiritually.

- Actively prevent fatigue

Rest before you get tired or weary. Call for back-up or support to watch your loved one while you rest. Enroll them in adult day care or sign them into a respite facility for the weekend if there is no other option, imagining packing any guilt into a tight bag and tossing it out with the trash. Remember this, when your body is ready to rest, it will enter that rest with you or without you. Rest, because you must, but don't quit.

CHAPTER 4 PLAY: MAKE YOURSELF HAPPY

"Sometimes it's important to work for that pot of gold. But other times it's essential to take time off and to make sure that your most important decision in the day simply consists of choosing which color to slide down on the rainbow." ~ Douglas Pagels, These Are the Gifts I'd Like to Give to You

"Happy during the day light hours, happy during the darkness that follows, happy to be free to be… And know my happiness depends on me."

~ Poem by Madeleine Carol Evans Tinsley

In my opinion to be happy is to be healthier. When greeting people and they ask me how am I doing I answer "Sensational," and

98.7% of the time I truly am. If my emotions are sagging just a bit, I can begin to go inside and count the reasons why I am sensational. That actions tends to lift my spirit and remind me of the blessings I have been afforded such as being able to think about the sensational things in my life. That makes my heart happy.

Inside of our world of "dementia drama" and sharing our love and energy in challenging circumstances, we can truly benefit from all of the happiness we can get.

According to Positive Psychology, scientific studies have begun to reveal a host of physical health benefits surrounding happiness, including a stronger immune system, stronger resilience in the face of stress, and a stronger heart.

And less risk of cardiovascular disease, along with quicker recovery time when overcoming illness or surgery. They report that "research is showing bringing more happiness into your life has far more benefits than merely feeling good."

It was Aristotle who once said, "Happiness is the meaning and purpose of life, the whole aim and the end of human existence" – a sentiment that is still true today. There is a range of science and research to back it up.

As caregivers it is vital that we are overflowing our cups so that we can help to bring joy and happiness to our loved ones as well as ourselves.

Here are some things to think about regarding making yourself happy:

• Think of the people in your life that you love and respect. How do you treat them?

You are kind to them, patient with their thoughts and ideas, and you forgive them when they make a mistake. You give them space, time, and opportunity; you make sure they have the room to grow because you love them enough to believe in the potential of their growth.

Now think of how you treat yourself.

Do you give yourself the love and respect you might give your closest friends or significant other?

Do you take care of your body, your mind and your needs?

Here are some ways you can show your body and your mind self-love in your everyday life – which will produce happiness in your life:

• Sleeping properly.

- Eating healthy.

- Giving yourself time and space to understand your spirituality.

- Praying and Praising regularly.

- Exercising regularly.

- Thanking yourself and those around you.

- Playing – outside - a portion of every day, in a way that brings joy to your heart.

Coach Lisa Nichols assigned our tribe to spend time playing and take a picture or video tape what we chose to do. I purchased a bag of jacks (which I had a challenge finding), a jump rope and a bottle of bubbles with different size fans so I could fan the bubbles through the air and make rainbow colored clouds of liquid joy.

I must admit I haven't played with any of those items in a while, but I do have them near me. The jacks are right here on my desk as I type these words.

I do make every effort that I can to do something that brings joy to my heart and makes me happy every day, even while I am traveling and away from caring for my mama. I look at pictures of my precious little nieces, nephews, grand babies and little cousins I have stored in my cell phone.

I will phone a friend, send a text or write a card to a friend. I take time to sit and read a good book or watch an uplifting movie like "Happy Feet." L-O-V-E that movie. I catch myself with a big smile on my face and moving to the music while on the sofa watching it.

When I am with my mama, I will open YouTube, find Diana Ross and the Supremes, grab a hair brush to use as a microphone and perform for my mama, imitating what I remember her doing countless times when I was growing up. She almost always will dance in place as she sits on the sofa. On occasion I have been able to convince her to get up and move her beautiful self in motion to the music. It brings overwhelming joy and happiness to my heart and I believe to hers as well.

Mama is known for the tens of thousands photographs she has in an array of photo albums around her apartment. She and I will look at them together or I will lie in the floor and stroll through the precious memories captured on film by my "picture taking" mama. I have almost surpassed the number of pictures she had taken over the years. My family can contest (or protest) to that. (Lol)

There is a classic book titled "Simple Abundance: A Daybook of Comfort and Joy" by Sarah Ban Breathnach. It is described as "a book of evocative essays, one for every day of the year. It shows you how your daily life can be an expression of your authentic self.

Every day, your own true path will lead you to a happier, more fulfilling, and contented way of life." At the end of each month's daily motivating essays, Sarah offers "Joyful Simplicities" for the month, suggestions of simple creative things to do to bring you authentic joy and happiness to your life.

One of her Joyful Simplicities for December is "fulfill the holiday dream of a child who isn't yours." What greater joy can we give ourselves than to give to someone else?

As a caregiver, I encourage you to include your giving to another caregiver that you know. Offering to pick up some groceries for her during your run to the store; sending her a beautiful card or even a gift box of blank note cards so that she can share the same joyful kindness with one of her friends as you have shared with her.

Here is what my mama wrote in her poem called "Gifts:"

GIFTS

"Bees and butterflies, flowers and trees, oceans and clouds, and a warm summer breeze, these are just some of the things that I love, some of the gifts that are sent from above.

A walk in a park, on a warm spring day, with a child by my side that I am showing the way. The look on the face of the child is a thrill, it's so happy and healthy, and so genuinely real.

I love the little hands, as they cling to mine. These are the gifts I'll treasure through time."

Happiness is an inside job. Hire yourself to make you happy.

CHAPTER 5 PREPARE: YOU CAN NOW HANDLE THE BUSINESS THAT NEEDS TO BE HANDLED

"Self-care is not a waste of time; Self-care makes your use of time more sustainable." ~ Jackie Viramontez

The beginning of our family's journey in discovering something was cognitively out of balance with our mother was marked when I happened to be visiting her home from out of state and answered a knock at her front door. It was a process server that handed me a foreclosure notice for non-payment of property taxes. To say I was caught completely off guard is an understatement.

We had noticed that Mama complained of her cable "not working" or her phone bill being overdue and she needed some money until the beginning of the next month, however it didn't seem anything more than an occasional oversight on her part.

That assumption was corrected when the five of her children got together and compared notes on the money she was borrowing from us and the amount we individually stepped up to pay on her phone, utility bills, groceries or other needs.

I set up a telephone conference call and we discussed our options. We came up with the game plan for all 5 of us to contribute equally to cover the cost of back taxes to get her out of foreclosure. It was all contingent on her allowing me, her eldest, with the least amount of personal, family responsibility and the most flexible schedule to become Power of Attorney and "assist" her with her finances. She was humbled at the knowledge of her children caring to such depths for her and she quickly agreed.

All went smoothly from the hearing at the court house on the appointed date to answering the foreclosure summons, to signing of the power of attorney paperwork.

Yet things took a swift, downward turn when one of my sisters and I were at the bank with our mother, having my name added to her account and obtaining a separate bank card. Mama hit the roof when the bank manager explained how the Power of Attorney process worked.

Although we had explained the process to her several times she did not want anyone having access to her money except her. Mind you, this was AFTER we had paid her back property taxes and saved her home from being taken away from her.

My sister spoke up, before I could even wrap my brain around Mama's sudden disagreement. We have been able to get through this season by leaning on each other and taking care of ourselves, even as all the new revelation about Mama's condition began to clearly unfold.

Caring for yourself is a continual process. You have to begin each day with a focused mind and strong body to attend to all that needs to be addressed in a day in the life of you caring for your loved one.

Some of the items you want to put in place include power of attorney or guardianship and conservatorship. Consult your attorney or Legal Shield office to answer questions you have and to get a full understanding and wisdom on what is right for you loved one's situation.

Be sure to keep good, organized records and receipts of all that is spent. This will help with the annual reporting to the Probate Court. Most Probate Courts offer free monthly classes on basic training with practical information on acting as a guardian for adults and a conservator.

Let's discuss the topic of finances, yours and those of your loved ones.

It is vital that you as the caregiver have a firm handle on your personal finances. You want to ensure that your monthly obligations are being met and nothing is overlooked.

Automation is your friend! Have your re-occurring monthly payment set up with your

bank for Auto-pay. Before personally implementing this wisdom, I found myself on occasion rushing at the last minute to pay a utility bills before the service was disconnected
or making arrangements to pay bills at a later
date, when the budget was overloaded and
money was not available to pay it when it was
due.

Dave Ramsey, a personal money-
management expert and extremely popular
national radio personality shares this wisdom: "Taking care of your elderly parents can
be tough on your emotions and your money.
It's even tougher when it feels like you are
being torn between caring for your parents
and saving for your own retirement or the
kid's college fund.

"Having the right plan – which, in this case,
means saving for retirement first and then

college – can do wonders for you. A plan keeps you from being overwhelmed and making emotional decisions. Stay focused on the plan and stay calm. You can do this!

First get your budget in place and follow the 'Baby Steps'. Then save an emergency fund of three to six months' worth of expenses.

"…It's important to save for your golden years even if you are taking care of your parents. Don't overlook that. A 2015 study by the Government Accountability Office reports that about 29% of households with someone age 55 or older don't have retirement savings or a traditional pension plan. Being older with no money is not a spot you want to be in. Take advantage of the time you have now so that you will be ready."

If you happen to be among that 29%, there are still options to help you live with peace of mind and reach your goals. It may be a real challenge, yet there is always help and there is always hope.

I love the saying "when the student is ready, the teacher will appear." Quitting is not an option. You still have life left in your body to live as well as helping to take care of your loved one. Speak up and ask for the wisdom and help you need.

Regarding caring for your elderly parents Dave shares this: "This is the toughest subject because it involves aging parents and all the emotions that come with that. It's important to have two things in place: a plan for the money and healthy boundaries.

Healthy boundaries mean not letting anyone manipulate you or make you feel guilty. Emotions can run high when parents don't want to move from their home or don't have a lot of money saved. Grown sibling might argue about who should help with mom and dad. In the midst of all that, stay calm and don't forget to look after your own household.

It's common for families to pitch in a little more when the mother or father get older. A 2015 Pew Research Center Poll shows that 79% of Americans say family provides most of the help for aging parents.

If parents require in-home care, an assisted-living facility or a nursing home, look at their money situation with them (before latter stage dementia sets in) and decide what fits with their budget. This is the part that requires emotional strength. They may not want to move or prefer a place that's too expensive. Don't let that bring you down. You aren't doing anything wrong. This is not a case of you being cruel – it's about finding an affordable way to provide necessary care for your parents.

Talk through the situation with them using facts. It may take a while for them to warm up to the idea of getting help, so be patient. Any assistance you give while maintaining healthy boundaries is a blessing to everyone.

 https://www.daveramsey.com/blog/caring-for-elderly-parents

For wisdom on your personal finances check out Dave Ramsey at https://www.daveramsey.com/dave-ramsey-7-baby-steps
Putting financial and legal plans in place now allows you to help your loved one with dementia to express wishes for future care and decisions. It allows time to work through the complex issues involved in long-term care.

By helping your loved one with this matter you are helping yourself save time, stress and energy in the future. Also make sure there is a valid will in place.

Here is a link to the Alzheimer's Association that can be of tremendous help:

https://www.alz.org/help-support/caregiving/financial-legal-planning

I highly recommend completing the "5 Wishes" form for yourself, for your loved one with dementia and for your entire family. The 5 Wishes is a document, legally valid in most states, that includes all the instructions and information that you need to create a valid advance directive. I first became introduced to this document late one night while my sister and I were in the emergency room with my mama.

The 5 Wishes document is not just an end of life planning tool but can be used as the beginning of an important conversation. It covers personal, spiritual, medical and legal wishes, all in one document. It allows your family or caregiver to know exactly what you (or your loved one) wants, relieving you from the difficult position of guessing your wishes (or theirs).

To order the 5 Wishes form visit www.agingwithdignity.org. or call (888) 594-7437.

Visit the link below to view a sample of the 5 Wishes form:

https://fivewishes.org/docs/defaultsource/default-document-library/product-samples/fwsample.pdf?sfvrsn=2

CHAPTER 6 PRESERVE: JOURNAL TO REMEMBER WHAT YOU DON'T WANT TO FORGET

"When you recover or discover something that nourishes your soul and brings joy, care enough about yourself to make room for it in your life." ~ *Jean Shinoda Bolen*

My family and I are able to review our family history through the mountain of pictures my mother has taken over the years. We often find Mama looking through one of her many photo albums and smiling at the picture of the "pretty babies" or asking "who is this" as she holds up a picture of a relative or friend. Mama has a picture of her mother and her dad sitting on the coffee table where she can see them every day and smile back at her mama who is smiling at her.

Whether your journal through photographs, as everyone who knows me can testify that is what I have a joyous passion for doing, or if you prefer to record your thoughts and memories on your computer, I highly encourage you to document your experiences with your loved one you are caring for.

Memories fade and time passes often so very fast. By recording your thoughts and memories you can gain encouragement and wisdom for the future as well as bring joy to your heart in times of challenge.

Mark Batterson, in Draw the Circle: The 40 Day Prayer Challenge shares that next to his Bible, nothing is more sacred to him than his journal. He shares that "it's the way I mark my trail. It's the way I process problems and record revelations. It's the way I keep track of the prayers I've prayed so that I can give God the glory when He answers."

He adds that "journaling is one of the most overlooked and undervalued spiritual disciplines. It's the way we document what God is doing in our lives. "Write down the revelation." Why? Because we have a natural tendency to remember what we should forget and forget what we should remember. Journaling is the best antidote, maybe the only antidote to spiritual amnesia."

Mark even shares a testimony of someone he knows who created a "prayer map": a sheet of paper in her journal, with a verse at the top and prayer request written below. This is an excellent idea to help you to stay focused on your goals and to see "life" taking place inside of your life.

Dr. Caroline Leaf, a cognitive neuroscientist teaches the importance detoxing our brain. In her book "Switch On Your Brain: The Key to Peak Happiness, Thinking and Health" she shares the value of journaling. She shares that sometimes negative, critical, stressful or fearful thoughts just whip right through our heads without us taking enough notice of them to even be aware of what we're really thinking.

According to Dr. Leaf, it takes three weeks to get rid of a negative thought. She suggests that one thought is picked to be solely worked on and work to replace it with something positive.

She recommends taking 10 minutes a day to write down what you are thinking about then replacing the negative thought with Scripture, or some kind of positive thought or action. The pull to return to the old bad habits of thinking is said to be strong, yet the longer you resist and actively practice the new thought, the stronger the new thought pattern will be.

This form of journaling can be life transforming as we work to stay focused on the things and thoughts that will help to keep us strong, in order to draw from that strength to help us better care for our loved one with dementia. It will also help to protect our minds from similar attacks.

"The shortest pencil is longer than the longest memory." ~ Mark Batterson

CHAPTER 7 PERSEVERE: REST BECAUSE YOU MUST, BUT DON'T QUIT

"An empty lantern provides no light.

Self-care is the fuel that allows your light to shine brightly." ~ Unknown

"Rest because you must, but don't quit." That line is from one of my favorite poems called "Don't Quit" by Edgar A. Guest. This encouragement continues to come to my heart and mind more and more during this season of my life. The array of responsibilities that are ever changing within my family as my mother battles challenges with her memory can seem staggering at times.

This fact from the World Health Organization is worth repeating:

"Dementia can be overwhelming for families of affected people and for their carers (caregivers). Physical, emotional, and financial pressures can cause great stress to families and carers (caregivers), and support is required from health, social, financial and legal systems." (who.int)

Consider this: Without rest and renewal something is bound to break – do not let it be you.

The "truth of the matter" doesn't always help heal the hurt within my heart. The truth of what is taking place in my mother's memory and her body because of the effects of the attack on her brain, does not take away the hurt within my heart of wanting her to be healed and whole again. It does not take away the desire to want to help her remember and being frustrated and disappointed when she doesn't.

The truth of the matter that I need rest for my body does not stop me from wanting to do everything for my precious mama, because I know it will get done in the most excellent way to honor her, even at the expense of my own strength and health.

The truth of the matter is you cannot do it all and you are not expected or required to do it all. You have my permission now to remove that burden from your shoulders.

You have my permission to remove the cloak of the martyr and surrender to the vulnerability of being a mere human with needs and emotions that are programed inside of you to be met.

There are times that are easier than others to step away from my mother. For instance, when she is calling me a liar for saying that I am her daughter and stuck on the fact that she is "tired of all of the lies," or when she is laughing at me, threatening to put me in the mental hospital for stating that my daddy was indeed my father or that she actually did give birth to me and my siblings.

And yet there are the precious moments when I want to press through and do even more for her, when my dear mama proclaims, seemingly out of nowhere, "I am always happy when you spend time with me." "I am thankful to God for giving you to me as my daughter."

The roller coaster of emotions that we as caregivers spend on our loved ones can be trying, to say the least. However, one of the major benefits of being able to care for our loved one with Dementia or Alzheimer's is that we as caregivers can experience the beating heart of that loved one.

Through all the tears, frustration, prayers and seemingly endless duties, the opportunity to share precious moments of love and tenderness, even if ever so brief, is far better than us having only memories and pictures of our loved one that has passed away.

And yet, as we mentally prepare ourselves for the day when they do transition from life to eternal life, we can be encouraged by this thought:

"But in all of the sadness, when you're feeling that your heart is empty, and lacking, you've got to remember that grief isn't the absence of love. Grief is the proof that love is still there." ~ Tessa Shaffer

Using the oxygen mask example from airline safety demonstration, the oxygen masks only deploy when the plane loses pressure. Planes flying above 10,000 feet need to pressurize the cabin so that they can maintain a high enough oxygen level for everyone onboard to function.

A normally functioning plane, once sealed off at the gate, will automatically raise the pressure inside smoothly as the pressure outside drops, so that ideally you don't notice it much. The same thing happens in reverse at the other end to bring everything back to normal.

A decompression is a loss of cabin pressure. There are two types of decompressions on an airplane; Rapid/Explosive and Slow. Some of the physical things that happen in a Rapid/Explosive decompression are:

- Explosive noise followed by a rapid movement of cabin air towards the hole;

- This rush of air will carry paper, loose clothing, dirt and other light objects lying in its path;

- There will be noticeable sudden decrease in cabin air temperature with a distinctive fogging caused by moisture condensation in the expanding cabin atmosphere;

- The decompression may cause structural damage to the aircraft.

The primary danger in a slow decompression is if the signs are not recognized in time to take action to prevent hypoxia. Momentary daze, confusion and disorganization can be felt.

When pressure is lost inside of the cabin, those on board, passengers and crew, have as little as 18 seconds of "useful consciousness" (the amount of time in which a person is able to effectively or adequately perform active functions without a sufficient supplemental oxygen.) Once the euphoria is over, hypoxia renders one unconscious and can cause brain damage or death.

There is a significant period of time between when the oxygen masks deploy and when the aircraft levels off below ten thousand feet, the cabin re-pressurizes, and normal breathing can resume, without the aid of the oxygen mask. During that time the only safe thing that can be done is to grab the closest oxygen mask, sit down, secure your seatbelt and hold on.

Relating this to our loved one with dementia, when they become agitated, upset, frustrated or angry, that they could "decompress," may resemble this:

• Explosive yelling and shouting followed by a rapid shift of tension felt and a lack of peace and calm in the surrounding areas;

• This shift of tension in the "air" can cause temper-tandems, the hurling of vocal insults, foul language, and even throwing objects across the room;

There will be noticeable sudden decrease in cooperation from the loved one, along with a distinctive fogging in their thinking and speaking process, caused by raising frustration and confusion they are experiencing; This melt down and decompressing of the loved one with dementia may cause physical and or emotional harm.

During this time with our loved one, the only safe thing that can be done is to mentally grab the closest oxygen mask, implement the "4-7-8" breathing tip. (See Appendix 1) Sit down, mentally secure your seatbelt by saying a silent prayer, be still and hold on. Remind yourself this too will pass.

I recall one weekend when my sister, brother-in-law and I were staying with my mama. My brother-in-law was frying fish and boiling fresh green beans in a pot on the stove. For some unknown reason, my mama bombarded her way into the kitchen and demanded to have something to eat.

We explained that it was almost ready, and we would be eating soon. She did not accept our answer, grabbed a bowl from the cabinet, the ceramic spoon holder from the center of the stove and dipped it into the pot of boiling green beans.

We had respectfully stood aside to see what she was going to do, but from a place of shock when we saw her pick up the ceramic spoon holder from the center of the stove in the flash of the eye, we each went into immediate action to block her from putting the uncooked green beans into her bowl.

What had previously been moments of laughter and joyful conversation had suddenly and unexpectedly turned into a "decompression" in the kitchen, where she began screaming at the top of her lungs, scratching at our arms to get to the stove we were blocking, demanding to dip the ceramic spoon holder in the pot with the frying fish.

It took the 3 of us to patiently block our mama from the stove, while processing through a hailstorm of emotions and disbelief at what we were witnessing.

I recall a story of my cousin Aretha being literally backed into the corner of my grandma's bed during her shift of caring for grandma. I did not get all the details, except that my cousin, a grown woman, was crouching to defend herself in the corner of our grandma's bed as she shed real tears, crying out for help.

Aretha was being physically attacked by someone she loved and respected and would never even consider raising her hand or even the appearance of fighting back, at the same time of fighting back disbelief, shock, sadness and living grief as she witnessed a stranger who had invaded her grandmother's body. Instead of loving and hugging her granddaughter as she had on so many occasions, now this tiny woman in stature was beating the "stew beans" out of someone she would have laid her life down to protect.

It takes physical, mental and emotional stamina to handle and process in real time the disruption that often occurs out of the seeming blue in the behavior of our loved ones with dementia.

To you and all who are serving in the role of a caregiver, in any capacity, I encourage you to take time to rest in order to recharge your strength, mental and emotional stamina as well as your focus as you continue to care for the precious soul you have been blessed to be entrusted with.

Without proper rest and renewal, something is bound to break. Don't let it be you.

At age 64, B Smith was diagnosed with early onset Alzheimer's Disease. B. Smith is a multi-media pioneer in the lifestyle and entertaining realm; the first African American woman to become a national arbiter of taste, with an audience that cut across all racial and ethnic lines. Her husband Dan shares this truth, in their candid book "Before I Forget: Love, Hope, Help, And Acceptance in Our Fight Against Alzheimer", by B. Smith and Dan Gasby:

"...I thought I could do it all myself. That, I've since learned, is an all-too-common syndrome for caregivers. Going it alone doesn't make you a hero. It just wears you down, and burns you out, so that you can't be the caregiver you need to be."

I share this information with you to reinforce the need for rest in every area of your life.

It is especially important to rest if you are afforded the blessed opportunity to care for the precious soul of a loved one with dementia. Remember, rest includes sleep but also time taken alone and with others, that helps a person to recharge or restore themselves.

For additional help and to take a deeper dive on taking care of YOU, join me for my one-on-one Self-Care Strategy Sessions. As a result of attending my Self-Care Strategy Sessions (via video conferencing), you as a caregiver will be better equipped to have positive, productive communication and interactions, helping you provide effective care that reduces challenges for all concerned.

My Self-Care Strategy Sessions are for caregivers who are ready for effective ways to provide support, improve care relations and secure an accurate understanding of your own personal needs first, in order to provide the best possible care for those you love and serve.

Please remember to rest in order to recharge. Rest because you must, but don't quit. Quitting is not an option. You are needed by your loved one in this season of life. You are deserving of experiencing all of the love, joy here on earth, and peace of mind that God has ordained for you since the beginning of time.

Remember to:

- Begin by loving yourself first so that you can effectively love your loved one.

- Tap into your Spiritual GPS: God's Power System for personal guidance.

- Overflow your cup and serve from your saucer.

- Leave spaces for detours as you map out your plans.

- Make yourself Happy.

- Know that you are equipped to handle all that needs to be handled.

- Journal to remember what you don't want to forget. And most importantly

- Rest because you must, but don't quit.

Written with love, because I Care about YOU.

APPENDIX 1 - FIRST THINGS FIRST CHECK LIST: WHAT DO I DO NOW?

When you first suspect a loved one has a challenge with their memory or you have just received confirmation from their doctor, here are some tips to help you process through the initial shock and stress of it all:

1.   Ask for God's help. Silently pray, beginning with the 23rd Psalm, The

      Lord's prayer or even a simple prayer of JESUS, PLEASE HELP ME, NOW!

2.   Breathe, deeply. "Your breathing is

your greatest friend. Return to it in all your troubles and you will find comfort and guidance." Use the 4-7-8 count relaxing Method:

- Empty the lungs of air

- Breathe in quietly through the nose for 4 seconds

- Hold the breath for a count of 7 seconds

- Exhale forcefully through the mouth, pursing the lips and making a "whoosh" sound, for 8 seconds

- Repeat the cycle up to 4 times

3. Consciously take a moment to feel the earth under your feet. Ground yourself. Recognize that you are still able to stand, even if you have to take a few minutes to steady yourself.

4.   Allow tears to flow freely, if needed;
      even if you don't have a full under-
      standing of the why behind your tears,
      let them flow, making no apology or
      excuse.

5.   Take time now to drink a glass of wa-
      ter and eat some protein and fresh
      veggies. Add a cup of hot tea or cof-
      fee, in addition to the water if desired.

6.   Make time to assess your basic cur-
      rent needs:

      • Physical needs = have you eaten
        today; are you thirsty, how much
        water have you drank today?

      • Emotional needs = jot down in a
        journal or a piece of paper (trans-
        ferring to your journal at a later
        time) what you are feeling, the

thoughts that are going through your mind;

- Financial needs = include in your journal a quick overview of the finances you have on hand to cover you while you take time off work to handle what needs to be handled; make a note to call your employer and ask for Family Medical Leave forms, to put that process in motion, which will help to reduce the stress of taking time off work as the need arises to be with your loved one.

7.   Phone a friend. Call a trusted friend, telling them that you simply need a sounding board, or someone to pray for and with you. If your friends are not available, call a help hotline or prayer line.

8.   Do a group text, zoom or phone con-
      ference call line to inform your imme-
      diate family of the news you just re-
      ceived; explaining you don't have all
      of the answers yet, you just want to
      ensure everyone is made aware of the
      information you have to share.

9.   Ask for and accept the offers of help.
      Suggest specific things people can do
      to help you, as they come to you.
      Make a list in a small note book or use
      a page in your journal that you can
      begin carrying around with you in or-
      der to keep everything at hand.

10.   Purchase and use a calendar with am-
      ple room to record notes for each day;
      i.e. doctor's appointments, for loved
      one and for yourself blocking times

for personal R&R – rest and relaxation. I use the See It Bigger Monthly Planner, which is easy to read and use, the thin version, with no wire stem and 3 holes in the side to be able to put into a 3-ring binder if desired.

11. Toss out all guilt, shame, blame and fear – in any and every form. Know that "God has not given you a spirit of fear, but of power, love," and a sound mind. (2 Timothy 1:7)

12. Rest now, taking a short nap, sitting in a comfortable chair, or lying across the sofa for a little while. Pick up where you left off when you get up or the next day.

13. Rest because you must, but don't quit. There is too much life in you left to live!

APPENDIX 2 - WHO CARES THAT YOU CARE SELF-CARE QUIZ

1.   Are you exercising on a regular basis?

For most healthy adults, the Department of Health and Human Services recommends these exercise guidelines:

•   Aerobic activity. Get at least 150 minutes of moderate aerobic activity or 75 minutes of vigorous aerobic activity a week, or a combination of moderate and vigorous activity;

•   Strength training – for adults, moderate-to-intense strength training that targets all muscle groups is recommended 2 days/week

2.   Do you smoke?

It has been reported that your lungs can be very badly affected by smoking. Coughs, colds, wheezing and asthma are just the start. Smoking can cause fatal diseases such as pneumonia, emphysema and lung cancer. Smoking causes 84% of deaths from lung cancer and 83% of death from chronic obstructive pulmonary disease (COPD).

3.   Do you use alcohol in harmful ways?

According to the National Institute on Alcohol Abuse and Alcoholism, "Alcohol interferes with the brain's communication pathways, and can affect the way the brain looks and works. These disruptions can change mood and behavior and make it harder to think clearly and move with coordination."

4.   Is your weight in portion to your height?

According to the CDC (Center for Disease Control) people who have obesity are at increased risk for many diseases and health conditions, including: All causes of death (mortality,) high blood pressure (hypertension,) type 2 diabetes, coronary heart disease, stroke, sleep apnea and breathing problems, chronic inflammation and increased oxidative stress, some cancers (endometrial, breast, colon, kidney, gallbladder, and liver.) Low quality of life, mental illness such as clinical depression, anxiety and other mental disorders, body pain and difficulty with physical functioning.

5.   Are you eating three well balanced
       meals per day, feeding your body and
       your brain?

It has been reported that a balanced diet is important because your organs and tissues need proper nutrition to work effectively. Without good nutrition, your body is more prone to disease, infection, fatigue, and poor performance, heart disease and cancer. An article from Psychology Today encourages us to "Feed your body, feed your brain. Our brain depends on the nutrients from a balanced diet in order to function optimally. This function includes managing our emotions and our mood disorder.

Remember that one of the basics of mental health involves following a good nutritional plan: having three balanced meals a day of healthy foods including lean protein, grains, fruits and vegetables, and a small amount of low fat dairy and fats. Eating well-balanced healthy meals is one way to taking care of yourself that actually makes a difference in your mental health, and something that you have control over, something that you can do. Skipping meals or eating poorly can make you feel irritable, fatigued and more depressed. It's in your own best interest to nourish your brain in the most beneficial way."

6.   According to your medical practitioner has your blood pressure, cholesterol and blood sugar been consistently at healthy levels?

The risk of both diabetes and heart disease can be lowered by controlling your blood sugar. Heart disease and stroke are the number one killers among people with type 2 diabetes. Blood glucose or sugar is important fuel for the body, but when too high it can lead to diabetes.

7.   Have you experienced any form of depression within the last 72 hours?

Brain imaging studies have shown that brain areas involved in mood, memory and decision making may change in size and function in response to depressive episodes. It shows that the prefrontal cortex, a key structure in emotional regulation, decision making and memory, may also shrink with depression. Research supports that Chronic stress and anxiety can damage the brain, increase risk of psychiatric disorders. A scientific review paper warns that people need to find ways to reduce chronic stress and anxiety in their lives or they may be at increased risk for developing depression and even dementia.

8.   Have you met your educational goals and desires?

It has been reported that people who use the conceptual and research portion of the brain are more physically and mentally healthy.

9.   Do you socialize and interact more with live human beings, in person rather than virtually?

A study on Alzheimer's revealed that "we need healthy interactions with others. It shows that social isolation or having a few interactions with others, is associated with an increased risk of dementia and cognitive decline."

10.   Do you engage in satisfying sleep on a regular basis?

Lack of sleep may be linked to a risk factor for Alzheimer's disease. It has been found that losing just one night of sleep led to an immediate increase in beta-amyloid, a protein in the brain associated with Alzheimer's disease, according to a small, new study by researchers at the National Institute of Health.

APPENDIX 3 - HELPFUL LINKS FOR CAREGIVERS

- Taking Action Workbook:

https://www.alz.org/get-media/da9e2ce1d73c-437a-be7c-d5761afd06e9/takingaction-workbook

- Healthy Caregiving:

https://www.alz.org/helpsupport/caregiv-ing/caregiverhealth/be_a_healthy_caregiver

- Tips for Communicating:

alz.org/care/dementiacommunicationtips.asp

- Caregiving for Early-Stage Dementia:

alz.org/care/alzheimers-early-mildstagec-aregiving.asp

APPENDIX 4 –A POEM BY MADELEINE CAROL TINSELY

Gentle and Steady

Gentle and steady the rain comes down,

Raining blessings all over our town.

God will bring peace in our hearts again.

God will do it like nothing else can.

It will be like a soft summer rain

Or the light golden glow of a fireside flame.

The only thing you have to do Is

to your own heart be true.

No one else can show you the way

To bring joy and happiness in your life today.

Be Blessed! ("From Right Here Right Now Enjoy!")

APPENDIX 5 – QUOTES TO ENCOURAGE YOURSELF

"Each day should have a clearly marked emergency exit sign." ~ Dr. SunWolf

"Loafing needs no explanation and is its own excuse." ~ Christopher Morley

"Sometimes the most important thing in a whole day is the rest we take between two deep breaths." ~ Etty Hillesum

The Serenity Prayer: "God, grant me the serenity to Accept the things I cannot change, Courage to change the things I can, and the Wisdom to know the difference." ~ Reinhold Niebuhr

Don't underestimate the value of Doing Nothing, of just going along, listening to all

the things you can't hear, and not bothering.
~ Pooh's Little Instruction Book, inspired by
A.A. Milne

"Nourishing yourself in a way that helps you blossom in the direction you want to go is attainable, and you are worth the effort."
~Deborah Day

"As you grow older, you will discover that you have two hands, one for helping yourself, the other for helping others."
~ Maya Angelou

"When we self-regulate well, we are better able to control the trajectory of our emotional lives and resulting actions based on our values and sense of purpose."
~Amy Leigh Mercree

"Self-care means focusing on our mental state as well as our physical health." ~ unknown

"When the well's dry, we know the worth of water." ~ Ben Franklin

"Almost everything will work again if you unplug it for a few minutes, including yourself." ~ Anne Lamott

"Our bodies are our gardens to which our wills are gardener." ~ William Shakespeare

"If your compassion does not include yourself, it is incomplete." ~ Jack Kornfield

"Accept yourself. Love yourself just as you are. Your finest work, your best movements, your joy, peace and healing comes when you love yourself. You give a great gift to the world when you do that. You give others permission to do the same: to love themselves.

Revel in self-love. Roll in it. Bask in it as you would sunshine." ~ Melodie Beattie

"Talk to yourself like you would someone you love." ~ Brene Brown

"…To prosper and thrive, we all need a little bit of "me time" to recharge our batteries; literally and figuratively." ~ unknown

"Caring for your body, mind and spirit is your greatest and grandest responsibility. It's about listening to the needs of your soul and then honoring them." ~ Kristi Ling

"Self-love is asking yourself what you need – everyday and then making sure you receive it." ~ unknown

"Knowing how to be solitary is central to the art of loving. When we can be alone, we can be with others without using them as a means of escape." ~ Bell Hooks

"You must love yourself before you love another. By accepting yourself and fully being what you are, your simple presence can make others happy." ~ unknown

"How we care for ourselves gives our brain messages that shape our self-worth, so we must care for ourselves in every way, every day." ~ Sam Owen

"It's not the load that breaks you down. It's the way you carry it." ~ Lena Horne

ACKNOWLEDGMENTS

"This is the Lord's doing; it is marvelous in our eyes." Psalm 118:23

I truly praise God for His faithful, steadfast love for me. I thank Him for using me to birth this book and for the transformational power and difference it will continue to make in lives around the globe. A multitude of thanks to "my blessing" a.k.a. my husband for giving me the space to spread my wings. To my siblings, thank you for being a reminder of God's love in action. To the awesome Steve and Kathy Kidd, thank you for sharing your wisdom and encouragement helping me to help others make a difference. To my editing team, Odi Adelakun, Brenetia Adams-Robinson and Dr. Gayle Rogers, the gift of your time and talent is invaluable to me. It will be counted towards the blessing of countless lives. Thank you! To the awesome John Crowley, the best flying partner a.k.a. world renowned photographer on the face of the globe! Thank you for showing up – on a wing and a prayer - for the impromptu photo shoot, on layover no less! To Dr. Alise Jones-Bailey, thank you for sharing your wisdom and supreme expertise helping to keep me healthy and on point. You have been a gift from God in my life for over 20 years. Thank you for absolutely everything. To my Tribe of prayer warriors, encouragers and genuine friends and loving family, thank you, thank you, thank. God abundantly bless you all.

Made in the USA
Columbia, SC
26 January 2020